ESSEQUIBO

by the same poet

Mercy Ward (Peterloo Poets, 1988)

Essequibo

IAN McDONALD

PETERLOO POETS (U.K.) & STORY LINE PRESS (U.S.A.)

First published in 1992
by Peterloo Poets
2 Kelly Gardens, Calstock, Cornwall PL18 9SA, U.K.
&
Story Line Press
Three Oaks Farm, Brownsville, Oregon 97327–9718, U.S.A.

**A catalogue record for this book is available
from the British Library**

ISBN 1-871471-34-6 (Peterloo Poets)

ISBN 0-934257-90-6 (Story Line Press)

Printed in Great Britain by
Latimer Trend & Company Ltd, Plymouth

ACKNOWLEDGEMENTS are due to the editors of *Kyk-over-Al*, *The Caribbean Writer* and *Poetry Matters* in whose pages some of these poems first appeared.

Supported by

Cornwall
County Council

WITH THE ASSISTANCE OF

SOUTH WEST ARTS

Recipient of an Arts Council Incentive Funding Award

"To my Father and Mother
For so much bestowed
On their 60th Wedding Anniversary"

Contents

Amerindian

I think of woodskins, I think
Of quick arrows. I think
Of things Indian. And still
I think of their bright, still
Summers when these hills
And meadows on these hills
Shone in the morning
Suns before this morning.

River Memories

River along whose shores
The shadow of memories
And long-lost delights
Hang like morning mist.

No moon but one bright star
Shines in the black river.
Go carefully: there are rocks,
But the captain laughs confidently.

Jetty posts rotting in the water:
Boats once loaded muscavado,
Coffee, coconuts, and purple-heart.
A few birds settle on the black posts.

Blueness of the sky blazes,
A white-sailed boat comes near.
It is fast in the gleaming river:
Lettered on its side the name: 'Wind-Song'.

A girl in scarlet blouse
Beats clothes and sings.
Her voice comes over the water.
Sliding past, we turn and wave.

The sun burns on the cold river
Put a hand in the water wrist-deep
The rose-black water is cold and sweet.
Savour the two sensations.

Cloud-castles pile up far away,
A storm sweeps up the river.
Curtain of silver rain fast approaches.
The first drops gleam in the sun.

Hush and shiver of wind,
Chuckle of water at the bow,
Silence of green forests all around:
Senseless to say a word.

Stop in the shade of bamboos:
The creak of wood, rustle of leaves,
White orchids in the tree hollows
And mauve butterflies flying.

The river fills with blaze of orange:
Suddenly wild pigs are seen swimming.
Black and shimmering in the burning river,
Caught in a net of golden shadows.

River-beach with dogs barking,
White chapel in a small clearing.
A boat bobs up to the steps,
A man all in black gets out.

Green parrots fly in the blaze of blue.
Far away the river stretches
Into deep mists and mountains
Wrapped in shadows.

Trapped Agoutis

('It is good that the animal rushes about in desperation. The level of lactic acid, which builds up in the muscle tissues during exertion, tenderizes the flesh.')

Hardly silver light of morning;
Shouts of pleasure, sound of pain.
The lithe-running village boys whistle and cry:
They have caught and held a bright-eyed agouti.
They dig a strong stake in the open ground
And bind the small, resisting, pet-shop thing
So that by the neck it spins and spins and spins,
Dashing for freedom to the safe, green trees
until the stake-rope pulls it sharply up.
Again and yet again it makes its freedom bid.
It does not give up, it seeks the trees without despair.

The village life returns to peace.
Deliberate hurt is not the aim.
Nor is it thoughtless cruelty—
As children pull bright wings off flies.
They know the purpose in their blood:
Old huntsmen tell the sons of sons.
Past noon the rope has worn its throat
But not so deep that it can die.
The arc defining freedom's end
Is beaten bare and marked with blood.
The children walk about and play,
The women nurse the evening fires.

If Gods are good, why is there pain to bear?
What ignorance! To think that Gods are fools!
Of course they cannot interfere:
Before time began they made the rules.
Forgive the Gods that fashion fear!
Forgive the Gods that crucify!
It depends on what our souls are for:
Agoutis at the torture stake

Cannot know that they endure
Such agony for a simple sake.
It is not love, it is not hate,
But prelude to a higher fate.

When the village feast is done
Go out and watch the icy moon
However long our story runs
Man will not have his mercy soon.

It Is Good to Look Out on Great Rivers

Late afternoon, gold starting in the clouds,
Wind-ripples on the shining river,
Five rods down the bank fishermen come home,
Tether the boats, scoop water out with pans.
Children speed down to cling around their legs,
Are lifted up and shouting to the sky.
All about gleam fish threaded on long lines:
Good work-day and they swing the children high.
Food is preparing: sweet pots sing and sizzle,
Fat yams bake black on split-wood fires.

In a clearing of white sand under grass,
Near enough to smell the cooking pots,
By evening custom a rocking chair is put,
Dark mahogany carved with heron-shapes,
Stouter made than any house for miles.
Old lady, tiny as a doll, sits there
Dressed in black, white ruffles at the neck,
Sits and rocks and looks out on the river.
The hours pass, she rocks and dozes.
Sky and water stain with gold and rose.
For years like this she's watched the river
Every day before the dark rose leaves the sky.

She's not left the river all her life:
Her birth-place and her death-place will be a walk apart.
To grow to love what anyway you've got
Is one way to find an earthly satisfaction.
You get accustomed to what you've always had.
After a while you do not want to choose
Even if what's offered millions say they want.
She sits at evening in her dark chair carved with herons
And watches what she's grown to love so well.
Small gold flowers sift down at certain seasons,
Fish break the surface in bubbling silver streaks,
Birds flash down and up, mirroring themselves.
A song drifts across the water from some burly men:
She shades her eyes to see a little better.

What happens now has happened long ago:
The drama of the river entertains her.
Farmers paddle to Parika on the coast
With piles of mottled pumpkins big as boulders,
Mangoes rosy-gold, and green plantain stems.
Schooners bound for Skull Point's landing stage
With orchids, tractor parts, and drums of oil
Pass and hoot: old lady gives a wave.
Gold dredgers move slowly up towards green creeks.
Drunken axemen out of Willem's timber yard
Sing and holler across the silver water.
Strong steam-tugs pulling greenheart rafts
Push slowly, heavily, against the flooding tide.
Soiled and battered little boats drift down
Loading blue gravel quarried out of Monkey Jump,
Charcoal burnt in Makouria pits, sacks of cashew nuts.
Corrials carrying gold men and young police,
Surveyors going to Northern forest posts,
Shopkeepers bound for Bartica and beyond
—A tin of cornbeef worth a fleck of gold—
Glide across the sun-path on the river.
Sunday families in white put up black umbrellas
Returning from the small Church past Kyk-Over-Al.
Three women dressed in red pass rum around
And shout with laughter in their motor-boat.
Old lady claps her hands, she's seen it all before.

Men head up-river on a thousand quests.
Deadpan Amerindian scouts slip past in ballahoos
To guide determined men in teams of three or four
In long batteaus brim-filled with food and fuel.
They aim towards the dark interior creeks
To seek what treasure's now the latest fashion,
Still full of yearning to find the Gold-Dusted One:
Precious letterwood to make a cello sing;
Rough diamonds found in secret green-deep pools
In pear-drop perfection will gleam in metropole;
Fish with red-fringed tails caught under water-falls
End a-gape entanked in New York drawing-rooms;

A thousand grasshoppers, russet, gold, and green
Fetched from tops of balatar for science far away;
Ancient Amerindian herbs to daub on modern sores
And bat's blood to test for some new corruption's cure.
The cargoes on great rivers change and do not change.

The trafficking is only centuries old,
Old eyes near death see something more than that.
The river dreams beside the huge and golden forest.
It grows dark, still she sits and watches.
What dreams possess her? How the years pass
And she grows old? How should she prepare?
Out of the timeless forest, darkness nears.
Fire-flies fill the air, birds come home,
If children wept, the tears are brushed away.
Cold brings a low mist on night water:
With gentleness they take her in to sleep.
The soul grows strong on beauty
Like a child's bone fed on milk:
It is good to look out on great rivers.

Half-Man in a Storm

Upstream sweeps the storm past Stampa Point,
Unbanks the river and makes it like a sea.
Fat clouds, swollen black, billow up like hills:
The storm rumbles in its thick beard far away.
We sit in sun and view the black horizons:
Rain-curtains in the distance fall like silver lace.
Big wind begins to shake the gold-leaved trees about,
The bright sun gleams on storm-outriding rain.
Soon it is darker, the river grows uncalm,
A strong wind rises and makes a nearing roar,
It blows froth off the tops of rising waves:
A dust of flour-white on heaving grey confusion.

The storm strikes, howls, darkens everything:
Now it's nearer night than golden day.
The river looks rough and huge and live,
Great grey bear-coat ruffling the wrong way.
The wind is strong ocean-wind,
The waves crash on black rocks like the sea.
Towering tree-tops like green sails unfurl,
Torn and tattering on long, bending forest masts.
The house groans like an old boat in a storm.
We stand soaked on this veranda-deck.

The rain pours down, we can't see more than yards.
Suddenly far out a red batteau appears:
It seems in trouble, the sails are taken down,
It drifts and wallows in the wild sea-river,
Wind-torn driftwood at the mercy of high water.
It looks as if the waves are pouring in to it:
We run down to the weekend cabin cruiser,
Big and powerful and more than safe enough,
Unanchor her and go to save the day.
Even this big boat is heaved and smashed.
The rain streams down: the hungry sound of wind.
We steer towards the red boat in the waves.

The batteau nears, crimson in the grey:
The waves are tossing it, water's getting in.
Firm set on the steering board, in old fur cap,
Around big shoulders a black coat thrown askew
Black figure in a rough black coat at bay:
A single occupant, the captain is upright.
He grips the rudder and keeps it near his heart.
His eyes are angry as we come up near:
He gives a fierce wave to shoo us far away.
We ask him through the roar if he needs our help
And know as soon words said they deserve no answer.
He stares away, he grasps the rudder: he controls the storm.

And now a moment when the image sets
Which lasts a lifetime and will not fade.
Half of him is cut away and lost
His body ends in leather pads half-way up his thighs.
He seems to stand upright even when he sits.
A few words only he spares us in his rage:
'You are little boys. The river knows me well!
The river is my friend'. And turns away:
The tall black dwarf dismisses us,
His violent eyes are angrier than the storm.

'Stumpman of the river', fisherman with a dagger,
He's roamed the Essequibo sixty years.
In Bartica he's known in every bar and brothel:
Drinks rum like water and screws pork-knockers' whores.
'His fingers iron and his temper bad:
In a fight don't let him get the throat'.
Sells produce from a farm and trades in gold,
Owes no man a living, no woman dare give pity,
His real life is on the great river in his boat.
Not one day passes he does not set his sail
And take his blood-red paddle, settle in his place,
And hold the rudder tight beneath his heart.

No wild winds stop him, he likes the weather fierce:
In a boat he's easy without legs
He's dexterous as any man on earth
Hoist, unhoists, black sails in blackest weather.
The huge leverage in his arms gets him round at will,
His quickness awkward but quicker than a cat.
The great river soothes his soul and it is where
His unequal body shows unequalled skill.

Shocked like when a knife-slip cuts to bone
We fall slow astern, not wanting to be left,
Silent, amazed, gripped by this black dramatic man.
At last the dark storm hides his scarlet boat.
The image is forever etched: he turns, salutes us,
A proud man in his boat, not less than any one.

Caiman Fever

Cold wind creeping on the skin,
A shaking-ague deep in bone,
All night in and out of sleep,
Fitful skin-damp wakings every hour
And a restless dream recurring:
Huge caimans thrashing in the river
Tails beating the water egg-froth white
Eyes blazing as they struggle,
Musky odour rising in the night.
I smelled and feared the grappling beasts.

Shivering in a misty river dawn
I meet Majesta who minds this house,
Ancient-slow but cooks a perfect pot.
She gives a look and knows the whole thing true.
'You have the caiman fever bad'.
(How can she know my deep-down dream?)
Her old bright eyes turn full on me:
'Caiman fever shake the bone'.
She has the cure for me she says:
Cold water from a baked earth jar,
A pinch of golden powdering.
A dip of lemon grass put in:
Drink it off in one great gulp.
Taste of woodsmoke
And old nights
Moon in cloud-scud
Red jasper round the throat.

The powder like a golden dust
She pinches carefully from a stone box
With sacred ointments and white spider cloth:
Caiman's penis dried golden in the sun
Scraped to powder on a fish's spine:
It's chased the fever
Down a thousand years.
I will not dream the great beasts anymore.

Essequibo Riddle Song

Bamboo hill is burning down:
Over the fiery trees
Children of the moon are dancing.
The drumming is gold,
The drumming is silver.
Thunder in the high castles:
The copper sticks clatter.

Look at him, so sensible!
That fine river-man
Handsome as a tall tree
Passes the sleek girl
With bouncy-bottom walk:
The bird stays on the branch,
It does not wet its beak.

Fish-trap gleams with diamond,
Will the diamond stay?
Sell it and buy a woman,
Will the woman keep?
Morning-beauty,
What lasts forever?

Last of Her Race

A walk in the morning:
Sun burning off the early mist,
River-bank ablaze with Lady Slippers.
Old hut in a green clearing:
No sign of fire-side or children.
Friends who know the forest:
'Come and see this wonder,
Maybe she's a hundred years.
Talk to her, see if you can get her story'.
Room is misty with strong tobacco smoke,
Old woman in a corner croons and drools,
Lifts up her terrible blue-stone eyes.

Miaha, 'last of her race',
Frail, desolate, decayed,
Greets no one in the mornings,
Relates no heroic deeds to anyone:
Children, children's children, not there anymore.
All gone, all gone.
She wears one green stone of Amazon,
Amulet against the snake-bite threat,
The gaze of Spirits that accuse.
A trembling voice saying nothing:
Deer have grazed for long
Over the rain-worn tribal mounds.
Her cloudy eyes skim past
Missing mine by centuries
Seeking something deep, eternal, lost.

I am shy, I am ashamed,
Edge out into the sunlight
Saying nothing to the picnickers,
Breathe in the green deep forest air.

Old toothless woman comes and goes
In this forgotten place smelling of orchids:
Past and gone, the wind whispers,
Past and gone, the forest hardly stirs.

A Stop by Cocoa Yard

A place called Cocoa Yard,
Scattering of shelters
Once was worth a name,
Not now: cocoa orchards gone.
Stopped an hour to get cassava bread,
Drink cold beers, prepare the guns.

Splendid things gleamed in the dusk:
Mountains pink in the distance,
White-winged birds soaring in the last light.
Lamplight like a gold eel
Squirmed across the river.

A pig's carcass chucked out by a bush:
Guts exposed and oily black.
In the skinned, earless head
Dead eyes are shining still.

River Grave

Near giant bogwood that blunts axes
Half-buried in a moon-filled place
They dug up chanced-upon grey bones,
Cluster of dog-grey bones, shining,
Out of gold and river mud,
Heavy, glittering, golden, clinging,
Old as mountains, there, looming black,
Far away, far in the mist,
The ominous, unsheltering sky.
Slippery as fish, silvery as river-fall,
In the bag that carried them to camp
The grey bones sang and danced and clattered.
Men the colour of honey and black iron:
One man hung a grey bone on his chest,
One man carved a grey bone for a flute,
One man boiled a grey bone for his soup
To sup miracles, to gain the ancient thing,
One man with a grey bone called the rain
To rage, to scour the gold down quick.
And camp-men used the grey bones left,
Made music with those clattering bones:
Hit hard at midnight all together
Clack-clack, ringing, clack-clack, singing
Strange echo, clack-clack, strange floating moon:
Old gold men dance and dance and dance
And dance, until old bones all-a-tremble,
They fall down, watch the bones still clatter-sing.
Whose grave was dug a thousand years
He must have been a music man.

Life and Death Tree

Along the dark, lonely river
Silent as leaf-drift
An opening in the cliff of white quartz:
A grove of dead-looking trees
Stark in the burning sun.

Out of black, bare sticks
Velvet-white blossoms spring:
The life-and-death tree.
Green leaves will sprout from it
As bright flowers die.
The scent of the gold-centred flowers
Pours out of the live and dead grove.

Four girls from the yam farm,
They are preparing a sister's wedding.
They throw up stones in the branches
Accurately shaking down the blossoms.
Their clothes are coming down too.
The dips of their navels fill with sweat,
Gleaming drops run down like diamonds.

Nearby, the stink of a killing place:
Black flies, bright knives.
Gleaming with sweat too
Three boys gutting fish
Marvel and fidget.

Carib Bones

Ten miles along a logger's trail,
Greenheart in flower smelling rich and sweet
A camp abandoned long ago
Has nowadays a few huts rotted by the rain.
Enter the chief hut by a slack-nail ladder:
Three old men squatting down like stones
Convey a welcome with their shrunken eyes.
We squat and take small gourds of drink,
Brewed wild cashew and sapodilla skins.
The ramblings of the old men grow wild
Soon others leave to hunt the angry pigs
And fish the clear, cold, black as satin streams.
The old men begin a chorused chant:
Memories of remembering their fathers' fathers' tales.

The old men squat scratching withered genitals
Sucking pipes of scented, strong tobacco.
Black tongues lick across half-blackened gums:
The chant rises, falls, whispers, shouts
And ends
Where it begins
And they are stone again.

The Caribs were the great ones,
Greater than the tall trees,
No forest men could conquer them.
Out of the arm-bones of their enemies
They made flutes to sing their triumphs.
Courage was dear to them as life,
Their war-songs sang of bravery alone:
No word for cruelty except for 'love of pain'.
Before they chose a warrior
They sliced his skin and rubbed in pepper bush
Tied him in a hammock filled with tiger ants
And if he made a sound he failed.

Fear they did not know,
Death they despised, a puny thing.
Battle was good:
To feel the heart beat fast
Was life itself,
The sweetness and the song of life.
The hearts of men they killed,
Dried in fires made of wood and jaguar bone,
They pounded into 'chieftain's' dust
To drink with shining eyes like blood.
And when great warriors died
Their bodies wrapped in snake-skin shrouds
Washed and watched by chosen women
Rotted slowly under suns and moons
Until the flesh was ready to shred off
Then women cleaned the bones as bright as dawn
Painted the clean bones gold of sun and earthen black
And placed them in honoured virgin-woven baskets
Carried everywhere, more treasured than a home,
Such great bones last longer than gold or settlements.

Kept forever, the old men chant,
Forever kept, forever and forever,
Forever to match their courage against foes
To guard the people against defeat
To guard the people against all ill
To guard against the giants of the dark
Forever guard, these strongest of the strong,
For however long forever ever lasts.

The Poison-Maker

Travelled miles that day
Gold savanna sun to shadows of darkest green.
A day of such beauty
I have not seen before,
The air gleaming like the start of the world.
On the edge of forest
Hawks hanging in the blue heaven:
Black wings beat once
And they are aloft forever.
They have always been in this great sky
Eyes scanning the long horizons
Where suns have burnt to black the short-grass valley-fields.
Amidst orchid-covered granite blocks of white
Gold and scarlet cocks-of-the-rock sport and fight.
Then the dense-dark forest green:
In the cold creek canopied with branches
The bright, dark-red water runs like wine.
Mora-trees, breaking into new leaf everywhere,
White, liver-coloured, green, and deepest red
Stand like huge chandeliers in ancient rooms.

Flashing messengers of light and swiftness,
Grey-blue kingfishers lead downstream to a village.
Well-kept habitations in a green glade:
Bustle with life, women bake and cut,
Children play with rolling balls of silverballi wood,
Hunting dogs snooze amidst the cooking smoke.
Red-stained hammocks swing in evening air,
Strings of red beads are heaped for market day
Making mounds of brilliance on the brown earth floor.

Relaxed, at ease, on mats of yellow cloth,
Chewing Indian corn parched white as jasmine buds,
The men extend an unsuspicious welcome,
Offer pepper-hot iguana eggs and wild red cherries,
Cool, week-old paiwari spiced with sugar-gum.
Their eyes are black and impenetrably bright.
It looks a place well-settled in good routines.

Alone, outside the evening light,
Alone with black arrows,
Who is that man, wrapped in black
Squatting in twin-circles of dropped black pods,
Crouched like a crow, stirring a black pot
Sizzling on red embers like a black cat spitting?
A chant of mourning comes from this figure of the night.
Why does no one approach him? Why so far removed?
Why will he never join the hum of life and light?
They shrug and smile like children who are happy:
'The poison-maker', they murmur, 'he is the poison-maker'.

Dream Island

Far up from the ocean coast,
Green-deep in Essequibo forest,
For briefest season—
Soon as fast-water comes, it will go—
The tides have tugged an island into being.
A blazing, bone-white beach
Appears mid-river, sudden as a dream:
Bank of sand and scoured stones,
Pink shells from pre-historic seas.   .
Low-tide you can land
And own this silent, lovely place.
Clear, red water lapping past,
Sea-birds alighting, preening:
The sounds of wings and water.
A great sky of piling clouds
And winds that are the breath of God:
Wide, amazing, perfect stillness.
I come ashore through gleaming water
Bringing a feast of gold-red berries,
Cassava bread, flowers for beauty
That will last an hour.
I come to read on this bright temporary island
The Overture to Proust's beloved book.
Heat-lightning flashes in far mountains:
Storms will soon wash all this away.
Lost, lost in the great river of this book!
Clouds of fire-flies burn as night begins:
No one will ever do what I have done.

A Trace of Sugar

One day, hunting wild orchids
And wide-girthed trees for corrials,
Deep in the thick, dripping forest
We came across strange machinery:
Cylinders, wheels, a vine-entangled mill,
Giant, iron, rare, calandria
Half-sunk in black and drifted soil,
Rusted nearly through and broken up,
A scattering of bricks that was a chimney once.
Black stubs of wharf-wood, useless and forlorn,
Jut out few and rotting from the river-shore.
Lost, lonely relics entombed in earth and forest.
And then, alerted, we found for miles around
Tracings of the furrowed fields, row on row:
Sugar's vanished, old plantations.

No one here knows anything of this.
No mystery why men gaze ahead,
Show no interest in what once was done:
Let the dead concern the dead.
It's simple to confront the new,
Choice is bitter in rememberance.
Bad memories only hurt again,
Good memories are forever gone:
History is soaked with sadness through and through.

Veiled through the tumultuous, sullen years
A vision of the past emerges.
For a blink of time the forest was defeated.
The bustle of a great estate arises:
Cultured earth and commerce burgeoning
Where silence has returned, melancholy, still.
For miles afar the cane-tops wave
Shining, shaped, and folded green

Along the contours of the winding banks
Murmuring in the wind that gusts up river.
Thick cane-bundles, worth their weight in gold,
Muscled in from sun-drenched miles aback.
Pure, clear juice spilling from the mills,
Thick black-strap congealing in bright pans
To make at last the 'honey not of bees':
This ancient sweet grass crystalled in the cask.
The barges fill with dark-gold muscavado
Loading out from jetties planked with ironwood,
Tugged for miles down strong-running Essequibo,
Across Caribbean and wide Atlantic seas.
You can smell it in the air
Stronger than sweat, stronger than flowers.
The wharves and storehouses, tall sheds filled with goods,
Mule-stalls whose scent is sharp of shit and hay
Fiery black-smith shops, forges, foundries,
Whitewashed chapel, rose-windowed, blessed.
Empoldered river, canals cutting inland deep:
Man's mastery for miles and miles around.

A narrowed eye which sees results
Observes this alone: energy and man's creation,
The forest cut, thrown back, and cleared,
River, sun, and the eternal wind
Harnessed in their wildness for wealth and power.
The absolute beauty of nature tamed and used:
The earth providing for the good of man.

What good, what men?
The eye of history opens wider:
The serried cane, wounds striped and stitched:
Man in agony, the coast enriched.

Scholar

The forest clears, socket of silence
In the huge green shout of trees:
Weather-greyed chapel, box-small, closed,
Dogs snarl and snap on long ropes
Round scarlet-blossomed trees.
My voice ripping the noon-day air
Summons the friar, frail as dried leaves.
Old age stoops him like a crescent,
One eye glass-white, skull clean-boned,
Teeth broken-black, his robe of threadbare blue.
He has never come down river.

There is no greater mystery than any man.
I see the old books I have come to see:
Shelves upon shelves in thousands once,
Latin histories, old maps, testaments and laws,
Thick books of traveller's tales and governments.
They all were brought from Heidelburg and Rome:
'A wild, green place for books',
He gestures in the lustrous air.
'It seemed a good thing to be done.
I meant to write.' He shrugs it off.
The books are crumbling, tumbled out of place,
Worm-holed, rat-eaten, damp-decayed.
They will go soon to dust like men.

I am allowed the old priest's journal:
Ten marvellous notebooks two thousand pages long,
Lined, yellowing paper half-a-century old.
I turn to April eighteenth, nineteen thirty-three:
'Rain fell night-long and in the morning
Gold-billed toucans skimmed the trees'.

The last note is five years back,
No more after. The old man shrugs again.
'To see the moon-blaze in the trees
Perfect itself. A clearer sight of God'.
The entries end. The rest is blank.
Dust drifts in the warm, illumined air,
The shuttered room is still. He prays.

'Hangman' Cory

When the launch sank off Fort Island
People were drowning in the black mud
Bawling out 'Oh God! Oh God!'
God did not come. It was like any day,
Sun shining on wind-rippled river,
Except men were struggling and dying,
Women and children choking in the mangrove roots.
People were running on the shore and calling
'Oh God! Oh God!' How God could come?
God can't mind everyone.
But look at this now! Look at story!
'Hangman' Cory arrive like God.
Let me tell you 'Hangman's' story.

Nathaniel Cory once loved a lady
She was a wanton lady, she used him badly.
His mind stop work when he see her beauty:
He was a puppy-dog in her company,
People laugh at 'kiss-she-foot-bottom' Cory.
This wanton lady take another man one day,
Open, brazen, she parade before Nathaniel Cory,
Laugh and say for all to hear clearly
How this man was the sweetest man for she,
How Cory never, never could satisfy she,
Nathaniel Cory stay quiet all the long day
Night came and when the man lay with the lady
Cory walked in open so, easily, terribly,
Lash both two with his sharp timber-axe fiercely
Cut them in pieces like red melons on a tray.
When judge-man say she provoke the jealousy
And Cory get only five years off his liberty
'No! No! No! No!' shouted Nathaniel Cory,
'She be life, my love, my beauty,
I have to go to hell with she, my life, my beauty.
She only gone in front of me.
Hang me by the neck to die gladly,
Hang me high, high and quickly!'

The people whispering make it legendary:
It so he get the name of 'Hangman' Cory.

Off Fort Island that bright morning
Was he who God send to save the people.
People bawling on the black stelling for a saviour,
They never expect to see 'Hangman' Cory come.
He live so quiet among them all the years,
Minding a pumpkin patch behind the white Chapel,
He smoke his thorn pipe, never say one word.
There he stood on the black stelling like a God.
Bibi La Fontaine, ice-pick thin and hard,
Fifty years trading plantain along the river coast,
Recount what happen that bright morning in her life.
Launch just left the Fort to go Parika side,
Deep inside boat-belly a thunder-sound was heard:
Time flicker, in a second, in a cat-wink,
Boat gone bottom. How quick it was:
She belched a warm beer she was drinking,
Before the belch belch good the boat capsize and gone.
'Under I go, the whole boat on top of me:
Mud yellow dim my eyes, cold log brace my heart.
I see my little Fancy who die fifty years gone by,
And then I see for sure is the monster death that come.
And my mind saying why an old woman should struggle so,
Let me go, and still I fighting not to go
And there is Fancy, the little one, crying in my arms.
A rough hand come and choke me round the neck
And pull me where I done pin good in mud.
This man had come for me in the dark water,
He find me like a miracle and take me safe ashore:
Sun so bright, earth hard, I hear a singing bird.
Never morning wind feel so sweet, you hear I give my word'.

'Hangman' dive and dive in the dark water.
Everyone like they turn to stone but he:
Women bawling and running and pointing trembly
Big men shouting and doing nothing foolishly.
Only 'Hangman' Cory doing the work of God.

And everytime he come up with another one
As if God guide him in the mangrove mud.
A score he save and still he went for more
Coming up with weed-tendrils round his head
And wound around his throat like gallow's rope.
He delivering up children from the river-womb,
His eyes staring red and cold and terrible,
Not one word he said in all his glory.

These are the plain facts about 'Hangman' Cory,
His day of evil, his day of glory:
He cut his beauty up like a red melon in the market;
God send him one day to save the drowning people.
Time will sort the meaning of all this out:
The hunting moon will rise one last, appalling, time
And he will come to rest like all men come to rest.
Though years pass, men should know his story:
'Oh God! Oh God!' the people call and God send 'Hangman' Cory.

The Satin Princess

In the drear mist of Long Island Sound
I think of the Satin Princess.
Hearing the cold clang of the fog-bells
I see again her moon-walk on the river:
All around her from the forest
The warm breath of flowers.
This clammy morning
Pale as ice seem the ladies'
Wrapped, colourless faces:
Their breath puffs white
And bitter are their eyes.
I recall the warm breathing
Of the far Princess.
She dresses with jewels:
The river fills with night,
Immense Van Gogh stars
Shine on her black bosom.
This pallid, shining world
Is bracing, bright, I know
But ah God! I shrivel in this land
Where life's laced tight
And unburnished air congeals.
The cold throws a spear
Through hearts here
Across half the earth
The Satin Princess moves and loves.

The Force and Beauty of Wild Pigs

Hunting night,
Clear as once was crystal:
Star-silvered forest.
Can life be ever better?
Luck with the quarry:
Quiet tracking through the thorned boughs
And then the hot, fierce hours in the forest.
Five great pigs caught and charging,
crashing in anger through the wild-wood.
The temptation of those that chase
Was ours as the black pigs ran:
When you have the upper hand
All danger is most sweet:
Life racing in the blood
Courses to its fullest tide.
They ran so near each bristle could be seen,
One eye close up glared red and gold.
We shared the killing all as one,
The blood and death of perfect things.

And then the good weariness.
Smeared with dirt and leaf-green,
Sweating cold in thick khaki dress,
The warriors sit to joke and reminisce,
River coolness a hundred yards away.
Morning begins to clear the sky
Bird-sounds start up here and there.
Pitch-pine fire crackles in a round of stones,
Curls of the pine-sweet smoke
Join the mist drifting between the trees:
The fragrance makes breathing deep and good.
Coffee spiked with rum goes round:
A brother punches his brother's arm in joy,
One man does a leap-frog dance,
All are game, all is play.
Princes of the high forest,
Princes of the crystal night.

Tough Indian Men, guides for the hunting,
Placid, squat, hard, contemptuous,
Bring in the trophies speared from mouth to anus.
These pigs are named as ugly. Why so?
The lovely shape of the boar-tusks,
Short, sharpened, white, and crescent
Curves in its own space: perfect tools.
Coarse, thick-bristled hide, undulled, alive,
Powerful, short, dainty-trottered legs
And the snout has its purpose like any snout.
These heavy beasts that stamped the night,
Broke trees apart like thunder in their rut,
Swing dead on sticks and cutlass-gutted.
Their force and beauty now are gone:
When they charged the forest shook.

Death and Burial of a Chief

The old chief is dead,
Born before the tallest tree.
The village grew around him,
Their great city rose and fell.
The names of everything were his;
The great river was not more important.
His anger was like a storm,
Water singing in the streams
His voice when pleased and gentle.

The day he died he called sons near:
'I am gone so deep I can see the stars
At brightest noon'. The spirits closed his eyes.
Clouds darkened at his death,
A cold wind lashed the waters,
Wild duck pierced the heavens with their shriek.
He had set aside a tall, straight tree
To make his coffin and its place
A hillside near the great river
Past the ruined fort Kyk-Over-Al.

The great spirits of the Dark and Light
Fight for the souls of men when they escape.
However good or bad the life,
The coward or the brave, the true or false,
The great heart or the meanest heart:
There is no certainty when life ends.
Eternity always is at stake:
Nothing begins or ends for man.

The struggle starts again.
Great spirits, entwined, contend
And living men must see the signs
When chieftains are at risk.
The village fills with fear:
Over the coffin the dawn-air shivers
As over a fire lit and burning.

Before night the whole sky flamed,
A dark red furnace lit the clouds.
Aloft the lightning is a fire-tree
Growing in the night, river-thunder rolls afar.
The Spirit of the Dark retreats. By morning
He has risen to high glory.
He has passed to his burning,
As they say, all dross burnt away.
The seedcorn can again be strewn,
And pure water drawn,
And new village houses built.

Perfect Roses

The belching saw-mill half-falling in the river
Stinks of steam, pulped wood, and acrid smoke:
It's near the hut which sells the axe-helves.
Far and holy, the stars control our fate.
The full-bellied lumberman scratches at his balls.
The slattern woman by his side,
Kimono slipping down a caved-in chest,
Slings a snot-nosed infant on her hip.
The yard-space slops with mud and chicken shit,
A cur kicked half to death whines in a corner.
They walk me to where he carves the axes
And where it seems she tends a garden:
Patch of ground, fenced with well-nailed wood,
Black earth neatly forked, packed with shining blooms
Sunset-red, and gold, and white as quartz from Pomeroon.
The pattern of a life is fixed:
Nothing prepared me for the perfect roses.

Dorothea at Work and Worship

Dorothea, in plain black dress,
Braceleted with black beads.
Beneath hair scraped back and gray
Carved, still face
Nothing gives away or back
Except a child comes near
And then it softens in a thousand smiles.
Spend a morning in her shadow
You feel the plainess of her days:
Days clean as sea-washed bone,
Bare of beauty, bare with beauty.
Tuned to earth and sky and river
As roots feel the wind that blows the trees.
Town-convenience scraped away,
Life scoured down to clarity.

Sun hardly risen she lights the morning fire,
Pulls in and guts the spiney mud-fish.
She visits the crop patch two miles away
Through dew-wet bush and hanging vines.
Amid butterflies like flying sunlit leaves
Gathers the pale-green, silk-tasselled cobs
And violet-coloured egg-plants, smooth and plump.
Returning, she grates cassava roots for flour,
Chews joints of sugar-cane for sweetness and strong teeth.
Batteau comes gliding under the huge sky
Skimming the river calm as mirror to the edge
Where green dragon-flies hover in a cloud.
She signals and the batteau-man lifts paddle,
Comes in with sugar, salt, and lantern-oil and spice:

Old Dorothea unknots her coin-handkerchief to pay,
Carefully knots it up again and puts it carefully away.
Next thing, to kill a tame duck from the pen:
Wring the soft neck with a flick, cut off the head,
Pluck the breast-down carefully to keep.

Noonday heat and stillness, storm-clouds pile afar:
Time to lie down in the woven, hand-made hammock.
Before, she shines a grand-child's hair
And cleans the pus from fly-infested sores.
Then briefly she purifies her body and her life.
She goes to the small room where she worships,
Rooflined with parrot-plumes and nun-bird black.
From a gourd scooped out to hold pure water—
Blood-drops put in from anything she's killed,
Fish-blood, bird-blood drops she puts in it—
She touches lips, eyes, ears, and nose
to praise things as when God begot the world.

Nightscape

Thin moon over water
Far thunder on the breeze
Eel-lights through river-mist
Cassiopeia caught in the trees.

Another part of history
A mad prince ruled the age,
At night each star he counted
A throat was cut in rage.

In time the world turns over
See! The prince sinks on his knees
The moon outlines his holy shape,
The star-entangled trees.

Explorer

Here men you meet are strange wayfarers:
   To find a tree that flowers blue in late October,
   Grasshoppers thumbnail small and crimson-winged,
   And ants that smell of citronella.
   Track streams that spring from black-rock shelves
   Aswim with parrot-eyed, ghost-white piranha.
   Trade with men who make the stonewood boats
   And carve amulets that look like pictures in a cave
   That scholars say go back ten thousand years.
A day I saw king-vultures soar higher than the clouds
A man came by and stopped and told his story.
   He searched for the lost Amazons.
   Soft English life, brilliant time at University,
   Rich family, smooth progress to the top,
   Then he read about the Amazon,
   The endless river and its secret tales.
   A myth had now possessed him wholly
   Gaunt, charred-brown, eyes like blue stones in a river:
   Ten years he'd roamed in every Southern forest.
While the howler monkeys roared
Like a wind through mountain passes,
He told the many tales he had pursued
To find the brave women without one breast.
   'I heard this tale of men-despising women
   They danced their men asleep and flew away:
   As they fly they clutch red peppers in their hands
   And pelt blindness down as the men pursue.
   Never to return,
   Never to return to their ancestral sway.
   Never to return.
   In a magic city they yearn and yearn forever.
   They live a thousand years and one,
   Their vaginas turn to twittering birds.'

Next morning in a cold and crystal pool,
Edged with flowing white mimosa,
Drinking cashew juice and sucking bitter plums,
Before departure when the sun was high and bright,
I asked him what the route was he would go.
  'A white horse's tail has brushed my face
  It is a sign I will succeed one day.
  Their sacred flutes will play for me
  And I will come across their place:
  Palms stand on guard with blackest thorns
  Long as a grand-aunt's knitting needles.
  A lake where all the gold veins run:
  It is not near,
  It is not far,
  The Mirror of the Ancient Moon'.
Mad as a torn shoe on a burning road,
Chaste as the stone I toss from hand to hand:
The beauty of God in every thing and man.
Gave him for his quest all he may ever need:
Onions, sugar, salt, and fishing line and love.

Incident Past Midnight, Bucksands

The house silent, lampless,
All close to me sleeping:
Deep in the night, alone
I go down to the edge of river.
It is a black night, velvet, no moon,
Only the stars spread like panned gold.
In the middle of the vast darkness of the river
A batteau passes, paddle-chuckle just heard
And a song comes across the pitchy water,
One man singing, not loud, a clear voice:
    'Holy is the wide river,
    Song of glory!
    Holy is the forest tree,
    Hear the glory!
    Holy is morning star,
    Song of glory!
    Holy is the forest tree,
    Hear the glory!'
The batteau goes down river slowly,
Slowly the song of the man fades in the darkness.
I think of the huge river flowing to the sea
And the sea curled vast around the earth.
I think of the river coming from the great mountains
Where it begins in small streams full of gold.
I look up at the black sky strewn with the incredible stars
And the bright net they cast on the water too.
At my back the immense forest presses
Heavy with the weight of a continent of trees.
Like a dream that came suddenly
The song drifts to silence on the immense river:
The towering forest falls down towards me:
No one wakes and I know myself alone.
I want to talk, fill up time with noise,
Speak with friends how we live everyday.
Something breaks in me, shakes me utterly:
To light the lamps, to regain the ordinary,
I utter oaths and sing and shout and pray,
Cavort beneath the stars, anything to flee
The measureless absurdity of the glory of the world.

Snail Painting

Cold-pale eyes, pale hair, gold-pale skin:
He must have ventured from an icy land.
Once upon another time for Sven Neilson
A pure, freezing country in the North
Must have been his stone-cold home.
Twenty years of wandering brought him far
To frontier river-town, deep in forest country,
Mud-drowned in late December, dusty hot in May.
Down a side street off Bartica main square
He runs a rum-shop where bush-whores and gold-men come,
Serves behind the counter and knows them all by name.
He likes customers to dance; claps his hands,
Jumps and jigs and jives in his blue dungarees.
I've been there and suddenly he'll stop
To play Mahler and Walcott's 'Joker' on the box.
He keeps green leafy branches fresh all around the shop.

One night he closed the bar down early,
Beckoned me to stay and led me in the back.
A long room lit by lanterns set on barrels down each side,
Casting gold-black shadows on a strange display:
Long, unrolled sheets of black cloth tacked on frames
Nailed to rough gilt trestles four-feet tall.
Eagerly and soberly he explained it all to me:
It filled his inner life, it was important art.
From a jute sack, one of bundles in a corner,
Soaked in water, earth-encrusted, tied with golden ribbon,
He dipped both hands in and pulled out a score of snails:
Gleamed white and pale blue in the lantern light.
He put them on the black cloth one by one
At all the corners. We watched their silver scrawls.
He demonstrates most carefully, anxious to explain.
The slow trails glow, meander, cross and multiply:
The tangled veins of silver make maps he can decipher.
The craft is where he spaces out the snails along the frames.
The largest works use up a hundred snails or more:
The black cloth glows in complex mastery.

At first he used to mark the movements on the cloth
To make precise record for painting on huge canvases
Stored for years, vast elaborate scrolls slashed with all the colours.
His soul being not at rest, he destroyed them all:
The snails alone are now enough for him.
He sees no greater art or act than this:
Such silver beauty, tracings straight from God.
Whole nights he sits and looks in wonder:
Immortal patterns forming in his mind,
Paths of peace and trackless wastes of war.
When daylight comes the silver marks are gone:
The day's first customers wait outside for rum.

The Card-Players

A paraffin lamp lights the play
Citron grass burns in a ring
Four men deal the greasy cards
Passing rum to keep death away.

How much blood does a man hold?
He gives it all eventually:
Last year it was the curve of a belly,
This year it is for river-gold.

The stakes are high, certainly.
The drifting moon, how old is she?
The ancient river full of mystery,
And the forest, dark and mighty.

The card-players crouch in their play
There is sadness in their eyes you can see
They wipe their rum-wet lips avidly
They want to keep death away.

One man beats his breastbone,
Another lifts an axe:
The scorpion and the watersnake
Leave them well alone.

Deep Pool

Just past that boat-killer, Sansom's Cataract,
Which boils the water white for half a mile
And takes the river ten levels down—
In a funnel of dark and green-mossed rock
Overhung with giant vine-entangled trees
So that no sun ever lights the gloom
Lies Deep Pool, cold and black as witches' bracelets.
A ledge of rock overlooks the still and crystal pool:
There's no hand-hold to be got down there
Should you be thrown or dive. The rock is sheer,
Slimed with water oozing like cold sweat
Upon the slippery moss and lichen-covered walls.
The drip of water in that silent place is ominous,
Sometimes you hear low sighs like women moaning.

A flower thrown in that water sinks like stone:
A skull will bob and float and grin.
From the tall ledge drop a severed jaguar's head
It will descend the black depths for a day,
Be cast up again with jewels in its fleshless eyes.
Let down a rope tall as all the forest's trees
It will never plumb those hideous depths
That have no limits known to puny man.
The taste of its black water strangles cowards.
Bring maidens late in bleeding there,
They will gush blood like a fountain.
Before ever man wrote down his pain
But carved it on enduring rock
The purpose of this place was plain:
Since angry Gods must be appeased
Here were they made promises and pleased.

A visiting scientist made precise surveys,
Succinctly described the properties of the pool,
Measured it exactly twenty fathoms deep
Which makes it deep, he wrote, but not mysterious.
Found nothing in it to account for miracles:
No dye, piranha, alkaline, or poison.
Strange sounds heard sometimes by the river-men
Explained by wind sighing through rock-fissures hidden near:
A plaintive noise, of course, but nature made it so.
He was content to note, in summimg up his paper,
That myths dismantled were his stock-in-trade:
He dealt in facts, not dreams and tales of men.

Deep Pool never gets the sun
And yet the moon is welcomed there.
The pale spectre of the moon is dear
To such places which shadows never leave,
Shadows that are made by more than suns:
Agony, horror, hate, and fear,
Not reached by measurement, are there.

Manateuk Falls

Jade-red stone below a sun-filled sky
Colours the upper stream rich rose.
Steep walls of rearing granite rock
Make a black and mossy gorge,
Narrows the race of water,
Makes it rush down fierce,
Hurtling towards the edge of precipice.
The river looks as if it boils with blood
Before it cascades down upon the empty air.
Rainbows flash in it,
The roar is mighty:
The forest round resounds to it.
Eagles mount the chasm's wind.

Here was fought a mighty battle:
Above the gorge the warriors fought
The greatest battle of their tribal wars.
Heroes fell by hundreds night and day
For days and nights no one can number.
Falling down towards the river's edge
The clash and shout and ring of conflict
Made the black walls of granite tremble:
The echoes reached the roof of heaven.
The whole forest howled with rage,
Vultures soared and shrieked below the sun,
The moon came up blood-red
And shone on blood-red death.
Bravery more golden than purest river-gold
Shone on that field most brilliantly.
The Great Spirits looked down in wonder:
For this were men created,
To do their fathers honour,
And die in glory on the fields of war.
The Great Spirits would remember them.

Myriads fought the mighty battle:
Of all that number, noble rank on rank,
One hundred were led captive at the end.
They did not surrender: not one still stood
When wounded, senseless, on the ground
They were commanded bound, with arms behind them.
And when again they had recovered life,
Taken to the blood-painted victorious King,
They asked for death:
'Not one of us must live to dishonour these that died'.
Their slavery would be the great King's triumph
Yet their demand was just.
He gave them death:
'Your glory shall live as long as mine,
Longer than the stars that have been here forever'.
The hundred were unbound and spears put in their hands.
In the corrials carved with princely emblems,
Those most treasured by the tribal fathers,
They took their honoured place, rank on noble rank.
The ropes that made the corrials fast were cut.
The river took them in its angry teeth
And shook them like a tiger with its prey
And carried them headlong in the boiling flood
Towards the tumult at the edge of precipice.
The hundred lift their spears in grave salute:
A mighty shout ascends the red and darkening sky.

In the white tumult of the falling water down below
You can see between the swirling mist,
The sun-flashed rainbows and the gleaming spray,
A line of jade-tipped granite spurs stand tall.
Like blood-dark javelin-blades prepared for war
These dark spears of rock look stained with blood
As if a hundred men falling through the roar of water
Had dashed themselves in sacrifice upon a jagged altar.
Who knows how many thousand years will pass:
Still the forest echoes with the mighty shout.

Last Voyage

Heaved up by the daily tidal push
Battered by storm-water and heavy wind,
The hulk has tilted on the beach of mud
Her rusted keel burns orange amid the green mangrove.
River-waves sprawl along the dead and gloomy flanks:
Sucking, vicious noises, her dead dissatisfied.
The slanting deck has rotted black and grey,
Mushrooms of fungus, white bird-droppings, stain the funnels.
Whatever din of passing traffic sounds,
Or song of birds from the deep forest flying,
A heavy silence surrounds old wrecked ships,
A cone of loss and long-abandoned hopes:
Gulls hover, shrieking, as if above a death
Or rotting food, their screech is ominous.
Each time I pass I cannot help but think
How once she shone at sea and came up river,
Full of daring, to ply a precious trade
Or seek some gold adventure far from ordinary coasts:
The mind's eye conjures up her spring time—
Ambitious captains in starched and braided uniforms
And sheep-skinned jackets turned up to the ears,
Sailors with fat bellies, sun-stained to mahogany,
Cleaning the caked salt, caulking with aromatic tar,
The wind swaying, tumbling, the mass of midnight stars.

Her end grows nearer by infinitesimally slow disgrace:
Every month she sinks a little in the crab-holed mud.
She goes to her grave bitterly, pieces disappear,
Mangrove wraps her closer in a stinking green embrace.
But last time I passed something had come over her:
Urchins ran up and down her crazy hull
And swung on yellow ropes they'd brought and hung,
Saluting, firing guns, and raising steam
Reckless, fierce, as sailors surely are.
Somehow she seemed sprightly in a tilted way
As if she might even right herself again
Come midnight glide out towards the Spanish Main
And, unfurling festivals of maiden flags once more,
Sail one last voyage to one last triumphant shore.

Forest Path, Nightfall

Paths cut last month to open up new timber
Are lit with streams of late slanting sun:
Beneath a canopy of green crowns of mora trees
Shadows gather except where float tall pillars
Of thick golden light that sets the green dark shining.
So evening falls, I walk this forest path,
Shadowy nave of an immense cathedral:
When Chartres is finest dust, this still will stand,
It stretches far, never-ending in its beauty,
Shines with its own green and gold-stained glass.
When a wind comes the stained windows shiver
A myriad alternating, dark then gleaming, pieces
That never reach the floor but float suspended,
Shimmering arcs of velvet-black and emerald.
One mile from here I found, below its cleansed white beak,
A swarm of ants eating the entrails of an eagle.
Night-shadows begin to rise, mist shaken
From hidden censers in this holy place.
Stars and fireflies, candles lit by ancient priests,
Fill the huge cavern with glowing taper-lights.
In childhood even joy seemed permanent:
I feel cold as if earth was cathedral-stone
Chilled for centuries before the age of man.
In this immense god-theatre night after night brings on
A sense of never-ending mystery vast as time
That swallows man, all his art and legends.
You cannot walk in great forests without diminishment.

The Sun Parrots are Late This Year

(for Chico Mendez, murdered Brazilian Environmentalist)

The great forests of the world are burning down,
Far away in Amazon they burn,
Far beyond our eyes the trees are cut
And cleared and heaped and fired:
Ashes fill the rivers for miles and miles,
The rivers are stained with the blood of mighty trees.
Great rivers are brothers of great forests
And immense clouds shadowing the rose-lit waters
Are cousins of this tribe of the earth-gods
Under the ancient watch of the stars:
All should be secure and beautiful forever,
Dwarfing man generation after generation after generation,
Inspiring man, feeding him with dreams and strength.
But over there it is not so; man is giant
And the forest dwindles; it will soon be nothing,
Shrubs sprouting untidily in scorched black earth.
The sun will burn the earth, before now shadowed
For a hundred thousand years, dark and dripping,
Hiding jewelled insects and thick-veined plants,
Blue-black orchids with white hearts, red macaws,
The green lace of ferns, gold butterflies, opal snakes.
Everything shrivels and dust begins to blow:
It is as if acid was poured on the silken land.

It is far from here now, but it is coming nearer,
Those who love forests also are cut down.
This month, this year, we may not suffer:
The brutal way things are, it will come.
Already the cloud patterns are different each year,
The winds blow from new directions,
The rain comes earlier, beats down harder,
Or it is dry when the pastures thirst.
In this dark, over-arching Essequibo forest
I walk near the shining river in the green paths
Cool and green as melons laid in running streams.

I cannot imagine all the forests going down,
The great black hogs not snouting for the pulp of fruit,
All this beauty and power and shining life gone.
But in far, once emerald Amazon the forest dies
By fire, fiercer than bright axes.
The roar of the wind in trees is sweet,
Reassuring, the heavens stretch far and bright
Above the loneliness of mist-shrouded forest trails,
And there is such a feel of softness in the evening air.
Can it be that all of this will go, leaving the clean-boned land?
I wonder if my children's children, come this way,
Will see the great forest spread green and tall and far
As it spreads now far and green for me.
Is it my imagination that the days are furnace-hot,
The sun-parrots late or not come at all this year?

The River-Crossing Moths

The sun rises on the silent river,
A few bird-calls haunt the morning air,
Mist-tendrils drift among the tops of trees,
The batteau glides slow on the quiet, silver water:
It is a time of peace and solitude,
The dreaming hour before the world awakes.
In a flash a cloud of velvet, shimmering moths,
Black-shining, edged with emerald-white,
Rise marvellously from the sun-touched bank:
They fly in thousands to the far shore.

The wild brilliance, the suddeness, the wonder:
Fathomless parting from all that is secure!
Here the great river is miles wide,
In thousands the shining moths will die.
Their brave fragility cannot last for long:
Already scores have lost the way,
Fall battered, gleaming, in the batteau
And flutter dying on the falling tide,
A destiny fulfilled to end without a trace.
The rising wind will tear their delicacy apart,
The sun will burn them in its great fire,
River-birds will spear them from the sky
For food or sport, or they at last will tire.
Their shredded velvet wings will strew the waters
For a moment, beautiful, then sink like sun-burst bubbles.
Rare and distant from all it knew before,
Will even one reach that green opposing shore?

Strange quest these velvet moths pursued
This silver morning on the great river,
Dared to mount the dangerous, high air
And fly towards the rising flame of sun.
On that far shore for certain there must be
A perfect lure to justify such lunacy,
A trap more potent than any life-force sets,
A poison sweeter than moth-nectar ever gets.
Some fruit of love, some paradisal tree,
In the far forest they discover and are free.

Ian McDonald is Antiguan and St. Kittian by ancestry, Trinidadian by birth, Guyanese by adoption, and describes himself as West Indian by conviction. He was born in 1933 in St. Augustine, Trinidad, and educated in Port-of-Spain and at Cambridge University. A keen tennis player, he was junior champion of Trinidad for many years. He played at Wimbledon in the 1950's, captained the Cambridge University team, and captained the West Indian Davis Cup team in the 1950's and 1960's.

He joined the Booker Group of Companies in the then British Guiana in 1955, and has lived and worked in Guyana ever since.

A novelist and playwright as well as a poet, his 1969 novel *The Hummingbird Tree* (winner of the Royal Society of Literature Prize for best regional novel) is widely used as a text book in schools in the West Indies. His one-act play, *The Tramping Man*, was first produced in Guyana in 1969, and has been staged throughout the region and in London.

With A. J. Seymour he was instrumental in reviving the literary magazine *Kyk-over-Al*, and he edited the festschrift, *AJS at 70*, in 1984. He was co-editor of Martin Carter's *Selected Poems*, and is currently preparing an edition of A. J. Seymour's *Collected Poems* and co-editing the *Heinemann Book of Caribbean Poetry*.

A regular contributor of newspaper articles on current affairs, the Third World, literature and sport, Ian McDonald has broadcast more than 400 radio 'Viewpoints' and 'Sports Views' in Guyana.

His poems have been published in *BIM, Kyk-over-Al* and other West Indian journals, in journals in Britain and America, and in many anthologies of Caribbean poetry. Eleven of his poems appeared in *Poetry Introduction 3* (Faber & Faber, 1975). His collection, *Mercy Ward* was published by Peterloo Poets in 1988.

In 1986 he received the Guyana National Honour, the Golden Arrow of Achievement. He is a Fellow of the Royal Society of Literature and a member of the Management Committee of the Guyana Prize for Literature. In 1991 he was appointed Editorial Consultant to the West Indian Commission.

Ian McDonald is married to Mary Callender and they have two sons. He has an older son from a previous marriage.